PERSONATIONSKIN

PERSONATIONSKIN

Karl Parker

No Tell Books 2009
Reston, VA

for Frances Joan Parker
now and ever

"Mirth is the mail of Anguish -"

.

"AS I FLEW ABOVE THE ROOM, I ONLY EXPERIENCED FEAR
WHEN INVADERS TORTURED THE BODIES OF THE CHILDREN
I HAD CREATED SO I COULD SURVIVE."

"If the eye were an animal, its soul would be sight."

" . . . the internal nature cannot be so far concealed
by its accidental vesture, but that the spirit of its form
shall communicate itself to the very disguise, and indicate
the shape it hides from the manner in which it is worn."

REJOICE EVERYTHING IS TRUE

COSTUMES FOR A COMPLETE DANCE

AUTOBIOGRAPHIA	15
AUTOBIOGRAPHIA	16
A DISCONTINUOUS GIFT	17
92° AND RISING	18
IN DAPPLED SHADE, IN BURNING AUGUST	20
LICKING THE SALT	21
I HAD MY HEADPHONES ON	22
SURFACE TO AIR	23
ORDERS FROM THE INTERIOR	24
PROGRESS UNDER BLUE SKY AND CLOUDS	25
THREE PARTS	26
PLEASANT EXCHANGES	29
GREEN RESEARCH	30
DESERT PLACE	31
A HOSPITAL-BIRD	32
WARM ALL THE TIME NOW	33
PASTORAL	34
BLUE & RED ROSES	35
ODDS AND ENDS	36
PUNCH & MOVIETIME	38
FOG AT MORNING	40
VIEW FROM THE LAKE	41
NON-SONNET AT MIDNIGHT	42
THE EARLY DAYS	43
THE RECENT TEACHINGS	45
DIARAMA	46
DAWN BY A FURNACE	47
INCIDENT	48
SHINING, STELLAR	49
QUIET ADVICE	50
"AND I [DANCE], AND / I [DANCE]"	51
AN OLD DANCE AROUND AN OLDER THING	52
THERE WE WERE	53
LITANY	54
RESURRECTION OF THE DEAD	56
A BLURRED FRAME, A SECRET	58
GESTICULATIONS, RAIN	60

SUNSHINE PROSTHETIC

ONE	63
A MOIST CHANCE	64
DIRECTIONS BY INDIRECTIONS	65
BEYOND THE LAST FIRE AND BEFORE THE FIRST I WILL SAY YOUR NAME	66
IN WARMER MIRRORS	67
QUID PRO QUO	67
DANCE A SLOW DANCE AT THE END	68
ANOTHER YOU ALTOGETHER	68
AN APPROACH TO AN ACCOUNT	69
TIME WELL SPENT, EVEN IF SOMEWHAT COLD	69
BUT THERE WERE HORIZONS, THROUGH THE GLASS	70
SOMETHING RIPPLING UP UNDER THERE, IN GOLD	70
A MUSEUM OF MAKING DO	72
FILM NOIR	72
ROTATIONS NOTED	73
AN INCOMPLETELY-BRIGHT SCIENZA	73
ON THE ECHOING SCENE	74
SUNSHINE PROSTHETIC	74
PLYING THE VINES	75
A PARTIAL UNITY	75
HOME	76
AWAY	76
PRIMUM MOBILE	77
EXEUNT ALL	77
CREDO	78
DAWN WIND	78
HORIZON EVENT	78
THREE PORTRAITS	79
SPECKLED ARRANGEMENTS	80
HOMO SAPIEN	81
WHAT THE LAUGHTER SAID	81
IN WHICH SAD LIGHT / A CARVÉD DOLPHIN SWAM	82
THAT'S THAT	82
THAT'S WHAT YOU THOUGHT	82
AS IF SOMETHING BURST	83
AMONG THE FINAL PLAYTHINGS	83

FORMAL ENTRIES & HORN O' PLENTY

DAY-FRAME, SKY BLUE, SUN BLAZING   87
MY NAME IS MUD   88
CUT IT ALL OUT IN LITTLE STARS   89
MEAT SONG   90
HUMAN WEATHER   91
FIGURE STUDY   92
AND WHILE YOU'RE AT IT, HAVE A NICE DAY   93
MANIFESTUS   94
GREEN THOUGHT, GREEN SHADE   95
AS SUN WAS SETTING   96
FORMAL ENTRY   97
HORN O'PLENTY, or, NOTES TOWARD A SUPREME
      CORNUCOPIA   98

NOTES & ACKNOWLEDGEMENTS   133

I.

COSTUMES FOR A COMPLETE DANCE

AUTOBIOGRAPHIA

That was prettymuch the story of my life
in profile. I keep thinking about glass, but don't know what to say
when continually thugs come to me in a dark alley
disguised as you, only a you made of glass
shattering back together. But all that's behind me now, I'm much better

than I was, a study in human behaviour of the particular sort
of person who says and does these things
in public, which is the region of my soul, O *thou.* I
consider this more like drawing
a picture of someone drawing
water from a well that figures prominently in a children's book
about the ins and outs of rigor mortis
and their relationship to fucking. Ouch,
or excuse me, I erupted again. That's not the right word:

life is scared. Dogs only rarely eat other dogs, it's just
a myth about our time, like the fish
that ate Pittsburgh. I was born underwater
eventually, wherever, found chattering in brightgreen reeds. That's

the honest truth. I work for the city, too,
you guessed it, a tax collector, but right, who cares.
Each sketch is action in a frame advancing
without expectation, in other words, without *end.*

AUTOBIOGRAPHIA

Hi. Since I just escaped from a maximum security prison
I have a little plan and am hoping we can
really work things out one of these days, but hell,
who knows.

I was originally incarcerated for my efforts to reassemble
I mean resemble—the prison.
During the night we were made to keep quiet, that was the dullest part.

Anyhow, once they tortured me I came out the other side
of the process pretty clean, pretty sane.
I used to watch other windows
from a wall-hole, my favorite thing to do each Spring as time
failed to pass but green appeared
calm as night in what used to be called heaven.

When I was a kid I had a cat. Now there's only
hatched plans and this, it's like trying to lick the dark.

A DISCONTINUOUS GIFT

I drive to and from work each day
in a station wagon with fake wooden panels
on either side, half-amused.

My name is Marvin. I refuse to die.
Plastic flowers are real. They endure.

When I was young I wanted to be
a magician, and make things appear
from nothing, like this, just

like that. A rabbit out from behind the found couch.
Feelings from a furnace, into which we push
our clothes. (This area is patrolled by moving lights.)

What I am is in appearance. It is not old.
Soon the radiator next to my knees is not what it was.

For these last recent things, I am untroubled, glad.

92° AND RISING

I welcome the fiend into my house
since his name keeps cropping up

everywhere, now.
My name's Regina. I wear glasses

and sometimes only one shoe.
This is my house, that means

to live here. Plus,
the people sway. They come and go

like people who just come and go.
My house is not alone, although

of course I must soon deal with the fiend—
he asks repeatedly for the contents of the fridge,

the only cold place left besides
the floor. I ask him his name,

the real one I mean.
He claims to be partial to pancakes.

I open a window to let the air out.
My niches will remain as they are

I tell the foul fiend already in awkward flight
down the stairs and out into

what turns out to be my new room,
where there are stars on the ceiling.

IN DAPPLED SHADE, IN BURNING AUGUST

Furrybody, curled; a ragged blanket
like old music over it, soft, worn.

Here we see such instants often
during the noise that means the street.

(I mean to cover here. I am quiet, still.
So many places see us all too well.)

Exactly as the undefined, the costume
fits. Heatripples, oilshine, rubbersmell

over broken pavement, and the conditions
for this instant jump another notch. Our

purpose is movement, as departures
distend the clock.

LICKING THE SALT

Naturally, if a body says a body it means
what a body means to it, especially
during, say, a stay at the beach
or some time in prison, where our codes
rarify to bone, with mammalian overlays.

We compete with subtle plastics for our lives,
for the forms of our lives, & find subtler ways
to congeal, agreeably. Overlays mutate
& become (single fingers sprout vestigial hands
and so on).

Flesh is endless, though bound.
No hiding now, not in rooms.

This pleasure is excellent, it bites both ways.

I HAD MY HEADPHONES ON

The other day on the way home from work—
I run a toy glue factory, and went by way of
familiar vacancies, not to worry—I missed my train
of thought. Hmmm. Sounds like a joke

a bit. Fine, I thread things through the rug at night
most nights. Not exactly happy, imprecisely sad,
thoughts around those words do excite me
to a degree. So anyway, the other day

on the way home from work I began to think
that it's not life that's like a dream, but rather
thought itself. I know, wow. All this was interrupted
(naturally) by the news. It appeared that

something stunning was occurring somewhere
and things were at risk. I decided
to pull over; vomited; got back on my bike
and headed home, but by a different route

which took me through apparently friendly
nonsymbolic woods, yet the sense of threat
was there, it was definitely there. I pedaled
faster, of course, by then the road was sloping

drastically but still I figured in the right direction
so what the hell, I went with it into vacancies
I hadn't at that time had place enough to pass
through awhile; they multiplied inside themselves, O yes.

SURFACE TO AIR

Rooms are where we do most of our thinking.
These are voluminous parallelograms
over which clouds pass, sometimes birds. Anywhere

can be seen from any otherwhere; all's narrows here.
I am famous & forget my point of view, though
I do remember other things, like dents

in the weather. Structures outside the home
through which I near you now, as if a harness
I'm afraid of, though it consists of various points of view

in which I feel at home mostly
depending on the weather, the daily news.
Maybe only grammar makes a rain of lingual

matters mean in seasons such as these, whether
nature agrees or not. No more now for now.
A scattered avenue—light rain—I become something else.

ORDERS FROM THE INTERIOR

(Not a bullet lodged in the back of an animal's
appearance; *the thing leaps away instead.*) You tie up the loose ends here
and let's get the hell out of Dodge. Have weapons will travel;
I learned that in school, back when. In fact, that's how I got to be

President, despite the fact that I'm a Catholic Roman.
Dawn is still my favorite time, though things aren't like that anymore.
I know you hate it when I talk like this
probably, but then again I didn't expect you to show up either

and truly (note the echo, ha), I'm glad all this happened
to us prettymuch at the same time
somewhere someone else comes close to knowing
action at a distance. That's what's taught in school today

which was fun although it rained, until I aged
and almost broke my leg attempting to scurry uphill, to the safe house again.

PROGRESS UNDER BLUE SKY AND CLOUDS

It's difficult to consider building a barn
when we still don't have a clue down here about the front door.
There is, however, a seemingly-endless amount of stuff

to get lost in, occasionally come alive inside (at least
that's what it feels like) an old treestump
or someone's accent. Some things are like treeswings

that don't need trees, and therefore of intrinsic good.
You see, we proceed by default, but don't tell that to the weather
or little rivers of flies start to stream from our education.

THREE PARTS

Begin

A gorgeous, dead bird on its back, eyes
still open in front of the school-room door:
shiny black and small claws
curled, as if with purpose.

Some of the rest of the pauses that day
were not to be overlooked, much less made up for
or avoided. Little by little
we learned not to touch every tiny thing

our shrinking hands still attract.
That was what eyes are for,
though the head lives largely underground.

Everything Else

Following the ball down the bouncing steps
down to where we all knew the school janitor

mostly lived didn't, in and of itself, scare
me; when he appeared, however, on the upper steps

with long black beard and hair
I was indeed afraid. My only option was

either to enter the underground guts of the school
through a dirty, though now-open

door, or to confront him directly,
which I knew would not occur. I was only so

worried I think because he never spoke;
later in my days I see how that's because

no-one ever spoke to him, so the feeling grew,
as everything around it did, too.

Like a Frame

A small cat on crutches hobbled up
to where we sat. Conversation ensued.

Its fur was small, with grey-brown stripes
and a tail. We talked about the weather
and general trends in each other's

meanderings—when a pigeon shot out
of the large, high, empty window-space
of a nearby building they're demolishing

(with appropriate, if simulated, noise)
from the inside out. When asked about
its crutches, the cat laughed

(but since cats can't laugh, what came out
was like that pigeon, only softer and slower).

PLEASANT EXCHANGES

He was laughing the other day as his young cousin—
in a dream, and in the very high winds often associated

(however unthreateningly) with his dreams—bent forward
allowing his grey, light jacket to balloon slightly

backwards, especially between out-turned elbows and sides,
saying This is (or It is) as if I can fly. The laughter

woke him up. A pleasant exchange. In the shower,
his body aging, he could find nothing funny, except maybe

some of its stranger, newer contours and textures.
Then it was time to work. As he bent down to drink

from the child-high waterfountain, he burst out
laughing, and looked around: the hall was empty, except for

one tiny cousin toward the end—difficult to make out
much less describe the difference between that shrinking being

and egress from the hallway which was by then lit-up
behind him in a blast of bright air, erasing us.

GREEN RESEARCH

An accurate sense of what a nightmare is helps no-one sleep,
least of all those who know this all too well, well enough (at any rate)
to decry it in public places,
echoey train stations and other avenues to human mixing alike.

Study the reflections of others as you are conducted, nodding, home, and
as a way of avoiding their eyes. This greases the wheels of the scene,
which vibrates accordingly. Across corroding distances, a wornout
funhouse grins. Someone opens up a map and squints.

Your mission is not the fact-finding kind, though it occurs in open air.
The more you sleep in private, the more daytime lengthens, until
dark is just the last and most anonymous mutation of light
in your later work. Beware.

DESERT PLACE

My accomplice is an animal, that's why I often have an animal's head.
We do great work together, when the stars work right. Somewhere

between us is the rest of the world—a spacious, spectacularly
grainy place in which I can be an animal, my other's head

and body walking toward me still, hungry, however,
calm. The desert where we live like this ignites some nights

like a bundle of rags in gas. The beautiful consumes us,
glad and dead.

A HOSPITAL-BIRD

A large bird wearing something resembling a hospital gown
flew, or rather sidled, into the fluorescent room.

The patients looked up, amazed and exhausted. It cast a pattern
on the far wall, the tips of its feathers were so brightly colored.

Soon the sick ones grew less tired, less borne down upon.
They wanted to shake its hand, and made as if to do so, until

the discovery, by some happy one of them, that the thing didn't
have what you'd call a hand, though

what was there was more precise and smooth and useful
than anyone could have previously believed.

WARM ALL THE TIME NOW

Morning, the large reddish bush—in the middle
of a small public square in a town that grows

tinier this time of year—glitters with masses of
hangers-on from last night's rain. One imagines them

evaporating as whatever will happen today begins
to happen, and sounds in the street increase. Still,

sitting in view of the bush on its slightly raised stone pedestal,
such imaginings—with all their little, glittery, liquid

differences—suggest there's no observer here, except
insofar as companionable accidents accompany the scene.

PASTORAL

To keep the mind
alive means to keep

moving, as in a field
where everything thistles

your attention. If
you look down to

be certain of certain
footing too long, the lake

evaporates and birds
turn clear. Weather

is a swarm of robins
here, along asymptotes

of blue. The grass
gushes, and slightly

menacing, its shores
divide your eyes.

BLUE & RED ROSES

You have to risk your life,
risk everything in a move as insane

as rowing across the lake where
the demon-whale lives, only to be

reunited with your one and only
love, if at all, in the whale's belly

where it smells of fishy shit.
The lies your love tells you there

will irritate the monster's innards
so much it will

expel both of you, either singularly
or together, at first

surfacing. Love makes everything
happen, as long as you risk

your life. In this land,
puppets and people are equally real.

ODDS AND ENDS

Punch remained at the lake
for the rest of the season.

Judy had made short work of him, despite the knife
she failed to sink into his bright felt back—

he saw it glistening and turning
out over the lake at times in dreams.

Daily hunting around in the bank for evidence
of the knife's nighttime presence, he came across

a pocketwatch and some used-up matches.
It was a sign, so were the reeds.

He spent the rest of the insecty summer
confusing himself with these sudden

things, then went on to create cartoon-strips
according to the states of being he moved

and was moving through without much consternation,
thank you. When the sun came up, his work

however paltry or pleasant it may have seemed to some
was finally finished. —The cabin spoke

in its own way in his ear as he sailed awkwardly out
on a wall-sized raft under twinkling knives

(A defunct pocketwatch with black matches taped
to its numbers, safe as an egg in his pocket).

Happy for the first time in what seemed like forever,
things like human birds must have approached him

in the dark, kindly, gently took pieces of the scene apart,
toward the expansion of their random homes.

PUNCH & MOVIETIME

He added, "I studied how to make scary movies
young, as a kid: drawers full of prostheses,
spirit gum, latex, braids of animal hair

adorning a feeling of inside-out
that learns and listens to this day
whistling (hum an old song to hear). So,

a wound-mechanics, brightly: blood tubing
got from a hospital, plastic incisors, headgear,
the awkwardest overbite you ever saw.

Among human festivals, October's shines;
or later, the off-white bones of a bird
in blue snow, a noise of something not going.

When the human monster removes itself
to the woods in the thick of the second act,
my disguise is how its so-called face

includes the woods themselves, into which
we still sometimes turn, and smiling,
hide a skin.

We are what thrives, says this place
jackals dance and scatter, after
eating, through. Alone, no scent is left

to the tracking, not a trace of fear, of you.
An offering, joined. I got in soon, came home late
(We are changed): would not be seen again."

FOG AT MORNING

Just before I go to bed, you're like a long coat
I can't synthesize. You make hardly anything happen!

Zombies appear in the mist.
They take you to the mall, where they make you try on clothes.

More recently, I've been having some trouble trying
to get through to you on the phone. Why is that.

Hills curl up behind my house now. And how we can see them—
more than you think—these last, late

few days . . . . We met at the disappointment
and draw our eyes together

sometimes still. A gauze; gilded events. I lay awake
asleep and twitched, almost lost.

We hear about you only through unspecified meeting-places
tonight, and the generalized noise of human thought.

VIEW FROM THE LAKE

Fronds adorn an edge. Some of them
especially are in between the place where I can see
& where I can really see.

There, there was no special purpose to events.
The days just clicked by one-by-one.
I am an extremist, I sharpen viewpoints.

Remembering my meeting-place was no easy task.
You stormed by it, you stormed by last events.

A view from the lake all recent things
feed into was needed, deeply

& emerged, in rippling liquid glass.
Anyday now you should be receiving a certain set of green
signals overcoming the grass . . . .

Down is joined by another surface, and
on the side of your face, when you turn away.

NON-SONNET AT MIDNIGHT

So many encouragements to your ideas
just lying around, practically growing on trees
as they say. Tonight you think to write
The moon was a yellow sliver—or no, The moon

was yellow, or just a sliver, for what it's worth.
In truth the moon means more and more each day.
Anyway, The moon was yellow that night
and it was then I felt closest to you, from that

imaginary standpoint in facts. The silverware,
once cleaned, gets put back in the drawer.
And then there's the whole situation with the mirror,
should we even get into that? Flecks of tenderness

twinkle in a wash of mostly gone, or never were.
Utilize the data provided, as night wears on.

THE EARLY DAYS

We were rewarded according to who killed the most
sparrows by midday. Slingshots, long sticks
and other things were used, mostly by small boys
who loved to compete (say, in pre-rain conditions
before the grooved fields get sloppy and the birds go
wherever they really go when it rains;
one kid maintains to this day they go underground.
This seems to our trained ears highly unlikely, though
it would have clearly served the little things well).
Our government explained
they were part of a general plague, and therefore
our enemies, since we needed to farm the land.
No-one told us their true function, and we did not
have the means to acquire such knowledge
in a generally-expressible way—though
many of the older among us knew, having been
threatened with long sticks themselves.

Once, one of the smallest and fastest kids returned,
beaming, with what appeared to be about fifteen
sparrows dangling in a tied clump from his stick.
Some cheered as the kid put it in the burn-barrel
where the rest of the collections were.
They gave him a badge of bent tin that had a bird on it
and some words that had become, over so many years,
impossible to make out, and thus
the source of many rumors, not only among our young.

Eventually, swarms overran us. Our leaders
of course, have never lived here, and so could not know
not for many years at any rate, how they had changed
the nature of our quiet at night.

THE RECENT TEACHINGS

The recent teachings have been, so far as
I can ascertain, strict commentaries
on the consumption of solid and liquid things
in addition to telling why we feel like trying
to touch lightning almost all the time
even though it only comes in storms.

Some of the more incorrigible among you
may scoff at these words; we are not afraid.
Two armies of our animal-headed warriors
have been told to station themselves to the north
and south of you, in case you decide you won't
wear your headbands, or say that you
hate playing games with the sun. In my opinion,

despite their great and obvious efficacy,
some animal-headed warriors look smaller
when they run. Nevertheless, I wish you all
the best—there is nothing you can do now
but breathe deep and decide to wait. As for me,
I think I'll have a bit of dried fruit.

DIARAMA

Encampments surround now.
My walls in tatters. Tell a tale of shame, of disastered faces.

They even have you working weekends now I hear.

Hope was joined in the ground. Everybody flowed.
Since we bind to occurring, this one's hard.

(I don't see how there's any hearing at all around now,
any kind of *even brief samples of real hearing.*)

These stalls in matter. Confusion stays.

Still a little boat without lights, still a throttled bird
by a child.

DAWN BY A FURNACE

Small occurrences shouted in the street.
Everything took place on a daily basis.

The words we used were part of things, however
minor, necessary, subdividing
presences. One afternoon I held a shout in my hand.

Today, thinking is finding
what to do in the turmoil, down the corrugated

hatch through which apparently by proxy
we're controlled in feeling streams. Our place
was always mending, and trying to find out why.

Still the occurrences shout. *My boss told me*
to go back to the barracks, but

I showed him *nothing of the kind was killed that day*
to the arranged amazement of almost everyone
in the mirror but me.

INCIDENT

The bodies were blown back from the tankard.

Drilling was hard going but at least it made work.

Someone was making a comeback. Come home!

Boys and girls turned green and were gone.

Time was when there wasn't any more of this.

That was soon or barely lasted.

Day came hard across the pointed tents; dawn veined.

Someone was making a comeback. *Come home.*

Boys and girls turned green and were gone.

SHINING, STELLAR

You were in like flint. Right there, in the thick of it.

You were golden, everybody died, they loved you, you were a hit.

Even the least among your means make us proud, make us happy, make us strong
again.

Might might not make right, that was what you thought and you know what you were
right.

You meant well. You meant very very well in fact. That was clear.

You were golden, silver, other kinds of metal. Certain urges surfaced, sheer.

Horizons glaze the eye. Redgold lizardshifting rings. Diamond mines.

There's shining, something removing, this thought burst like a vein
in the head.

QUIET ADVICE

One thing to do in a desert is stay quiet
and very very still, so only the inconclusive

stars are seen to move. From that point on
anything can happen, and once again does. Eyes

are too often their own points of reference
and let's face it, glad not to be elsewhere

for the moment, only small burnings
to tend to. Other orders pass over and

whistling in an ear, around. All the solid
accidents of scented air from here to there.

"AND I [DANCE], AND / I [DANCE]"

I have more or less protective and feeding supplies
enough to last me at least three weeks, assuming
things keep up like this.
The bombs out there aren't frightening

me as much as the kids. It's their torn-open torsos, their gutted
faces I can't stomach anymore. That's why I decided to hole up awhile;
all storms must pass, they say. My flesh in here
like glass sand ticks painfully, imprecisely through.

(My teeth've been removed, so someone else will know
I was here—signs for what's to come, which will not be
contained.) I keep my chin up, cool.

AN OLD DANCE AROUND AN OLDER THING

now that truth is meat to be carved.
What we see & hear on the news each night

designs to mean less than once it did,
though it hurts more & more

as time goes on. We tried to move
but can't. Onslaughts, & the thoughts

that splatter there keep us here,
glued as if to the TV.

There are no lights on in this common
waiting room. No-one sees the body

on the stained couch whirling in a blur of blood
& boneshards—the old inside-out trick, you

see—silently—where space is a wound best described
as universal. Still, the thing quivers

& becomes. We are made to eat the truth
each night now, though it consumes us,

its nightblue flickers. The rest of the people
in the remainder of the house keep very quiet,

very still. Overhead, everywhere, stars:
garlands of sparkling teeth.

THERE WE WERE

Then something told us it was time to go—
I can't remember what, though once I did.
(The sign was not unlike a sun in snow.)
We started moving. Meanwhile others hid;
perhaps they sensed the reasons why we went
blind on such a trail. Horizons watched us,
redtremblings just beyond our small event.
One night we slept inside a gutted bus . . .
We didn't know the place 'til we arrived
almost in tears, a sudden streaming, near
enough to kiss, like ground. Everything thrived
on us until there wasn't any fear,
no desire whatsoever for return.
Our place became the kindest fire to burn.

LITANY

I saw this through the violence that made it take place and we—
at least most of the rest of the people in the audience—were always thinking of you
there, but first things first: what came like a shock to all our falling. You were asked
to do something and then that something became part of you or you, wasn't that the
way it was, and if it wasn't it wasn't. I can only continually think of their flayed
faces, how hard it must've been to get the rest of the flesh from the cheekbones,
say—

Maybe there were other reports *but no-one saw you falling.* No-one wanted
specifically to kill you, to take your face. It's hard to be reduced to and remembered
through certain partings. I have been and am watching you,
from the first day.

I liked a little mouse because it was my friend in the burning. When they took the
rest of you and me out and called us long and thought we would burn like meat and
were right I knew they were wrong, because I was a child. They were simple, simply
wrong. Still, I hated to be burned. I hated too when you were burned.

My mouse said Yes.

I didn't like the way we, among the feelings, were left more or less alone. Now I
know why some hunt others and end them. It was included in the maps they taught
us in school, except they couldn't then see my and their own bodies burning in the
end.

I am sick of the burning, I made it. I am anyone, I hate to forget so long. I did what others thought. It was basic action, blurred in purity. Fire comes from the pretty mouths, clean. I love what I am, in the flames.

RESURRECTION OF THE DEAD

"An apple would lose its weight. They could weigh it and prove that a bug had eaten it. This bug made me get lost—that was three thousand years ago—and made the words get lost *so I must remind you of the gospel that I preached to you; the gospel which you received, on which you have taken your stand, and which is now bringing you salvation. Remember the terms* since they came from my teeth. I was full of bugs, and the bugs ate all the food. A big one was cut out of my stomach, and another one was taken out of my spinal column. The bug put its teeth into my teeth and ate my food. Another bug that looked like a wasp flew up against my jaw and knocked my teeth out. There was a second tiny bug in human shape—it was riding on the wasp bug: *This is the resurrection and the life. But, you may ask, how are the dead raised? In what kind of body?* There was another bug that looked like a ship. As I stood on the dock, looking around, the keel of a ship knocked against my jaw. *What stupid questions! The seed you sow is not the body that shall be, but a bare grain, of wheat perhaps, or something else; and God gives it the body of his choice, each seed its own particular body. All flesh is not the same,* which is why the words got lost. I was also lost. That was three hundred years ago. And then the bug made me lose myself again. But the bug was also lost. I used to have a bug like a lion and one like a monkey, *thus there is human flesh, flesh of beasts, of birds, and of fishes—all different. There are heavenly bodies* who took the bug away from me because there was *no room for it and earthly bodies;* and the splendour of the heavenly bodies is one thing, the splendour of the earthly another. Once there was a bug like a gorilla. It stood in my way, and I almost had a fight with it. *The sun has a splendour of its own, the moon another splendour, and the stars yet another, which is why I am afraid to offend the bug.* If I did that, I might not be reborn. *Some people are not reborn because the bug that governs rebirth is the one that has a head like mine and eats the food when it differs from another in brightness.* So it is with the resurrection of the dead: what is sown as a perishable thing gets in my insides. Then it is raised a spiritual body. I called it mine, the food sown in me. This happened after I went home after someone else's death. *If there is such a thing as a physical body, there is also a spiritual body. It is in this sense that 'The first man became a living creature,'* whereas the last man has become a life-giving spirit in service of the struggle with teeth, of whether other people have the right to put their teeth into mine. The two sets of teeth are apt to knock against each other. I went to the dentist once, because I felt so uncomfortable. Observe, the spiritual does not come first; the physical body comes first, and *then* the spiritual body. *The first man is from earth, but I do not like to talk about these things because I might use the wrong words and hurt somebody— you, for instance.* No-one takes me home for so much trouble. If my teeth eat food before it turns to dust, the second man can be from heaven. The man made of dust in the right way does not make mistakes in eating. We have worn the likeness of the man made of dust, so shall we wear the likeness of the heavenly man. *What I mean, friends, is this:* when I had the wet dream I thought I must have eaten green apples and that made the trouble inside me. *Listen! I will unfold a mystery: we shall not die, but all shall be changed in a flash, in the twinkling of an eye."*

A BLURRED FRAME, A SECRET

This body doesn't end; that means
no-one sees you.

Things appear, particular, material
events like sunsets from nothing, taking
forever to finish.

We are not gone by as people pass.
Part of this arrangement requires a hood
which has stars, and cannot be
hacked through.

Violence in our place means the seasons,
no more, no less.

The names in phrases we give these things
recur, are a matter of recurrence.

Animal-shines beside greyblue
waves, fur for licking here
& *here*.

Assurance is that
wounds suture, dissolve.

This page torn out, placed.
We do this in the dark like breath.

The thought that talks like skin
can't decide what it is.

Here is no decision, only little cuts,
or kittens.

GESTICULATIONS, RAIN

A fly glass-trapped in here sees
a pigeon outside.

I sit in a window, a talking monkey.
My little creatures move upon a hill

somewhere the weather is green
like trees.

I am, therefore I think
I am. Something's parting now.

The gentle ones are coming,
indivisible nonsurgical bodies, whole

patches of cloth, soft,
by streaming.

By skin and eyes, by skin and eyes.
Rain's a place that starts appearing.

The pretty people move away
& away, with a thought.

Fly not in amber. Pigeon, come in.
"I am, outside."

II.

SUNSHINE PROSTHETIC

ONE

Once we put the painted masks on, everything felt more at home.
It was like holidays turned inside-out, all a mingle of glitter and birdguts.
Something shined through our mostly circular movements, knives descended,
danced, the sun went red. Thought has a body like a blistered star. Now
we know how to proceed, down and in. Everyone has something special,
something different, to do. Some come and scream. I adjust the noise.
Seems like nothing ever ends, when we spread out, and out.

A MOIST CHANCE

There shouldn't *be* anything else in the silence; crickets intervene, of course.
So there's something in between the pauses, that part's sure.
In time, mountain changes are made. Now it's mildly dark, wires hum,
so come, let's away with us through this surface, peel back the skin, back
to the everything, the pale tenderest fleshpetal, where we are reeling still.
That would mean warm rain chanced. It was just that kind of night.

DIRECTIONS BY INDIRECTIONS

Slow down when the marshgrass appears in the field. Watch for last flashes.
I will be walking along the lake when you meet me. It's only just over an hour.
There's some kind of rain about my face I can't exactly understand.
And when a wall of earth came down upon me, it wasn't a surprise, dawn
clotted of its own accord. Somewhere, something is singing in my ear. Soon now
I am home. I will not miss everyone, at the end, I'll be there too, when
I sing in the deadlights along the marshgrass, which appear.

BEYOND THE LAST FIRE AND BEFORE THE FIRST I WILL SAY YOUR NAME

But let me for the moment content myself with saying privately in public among
amassed congregations of my peers no doubt that I do not set foot
one day of my life walking to and fro upon the earth as it were and *it is*
it simply *is* without some part of my being being toward your gone form, arm
in darkness, and so on and so forth until the end, or thereabouts, of time.

It is writ.

IN WARMER MIRRORS

The creature gestures, shines between things, the rest of this blistering day
doesn't end. Night's nothing but a low hum from the wiregrid of goodbyes
and getwells we are. Civilization's rarely surprised, hence its initial purpose,
once rains made even thorned things bloom.

QUID PRO QUO

Once we picked our way as best we could through the grass, found
not a single thread of hair. I must admit I loved you so much that day: breathed
by flowers, by the appearance of flowers. The same smells
must still be there. I can almost reach you through the ground, there's time.
Though I have to go to work so I can pay my rent, and return to you tomorrow
as today, picking my way through the delicious blades.

DANCE A SLOW DANCE AT THE END

So everything keeps or at least appears to keep moving, however tilted its axes
or tired you are. Tonight will be something other than the usual (however
affable) effigy of all that. Touch is the first thing we forget. Along
the long walls, bobbing, starlight softly-mechanically rotates, in a special blur:
a sense of calculated though genuine tenderness, at an infinite remove.

ANOTHER YOU ALTOGETHER

The fact that you almost never looked back amazes me to this day.
It was not your fault you were faught down in the garden weeds.
In every case I have playthings still, whose stalks have grown up *so*
they sprouted other things, heads with other heads opening in their eyes.

AN APPROACH TO AN ACCOUNT

Everywhere, divides. None of us may make it but I wish we all would.
The set whose members are millennia of winters (save one or two) upon your head
have brought no nonsparkling frost. And there's the marvelous lake, steel
halo in blue snow, now that the sun's gone down again. For which, these thanks,
for we are out of doors. Oh, I mean I am sitting on your porch
approaching dawn, somewhat cold.

TIME WELL SPENT, EVEN IF SOMEWHAT COLD

Since echoing it never stops ending. Things move through openings
in other things. At last one needs no nest. There's no exposure, no hiding now.
We part down here like dawn. What's the last thing you see.
Mine's a little spark out of sound. Happy to see it, to have seen it again.
Some strange kinds of friends in here.

BUT THERE WERE HORIZONS, THROUGH THE GLASS

The whole scene kept coming back together, except occasional frayings
at the edges, which we filtered through often enough, no cartoonland, no
dream. Dawn was just about the only thing we kept coming back to,
a feathered good, shining through whatever scarecrow or crouching thing.
A friend said: love is multiform. That's final.

SOMETHING RIPPLING UP UNDER THERE, IN GOLD

Staying in change requires force. For this sign we are equal. That sticks.
You mirror my mirror, riddle me thus. It's a glad land we're in, of a sudden.
It's kind when something like these changes comes of its own
accord, a glance across the look of darting birds. No matter the scarecrows,
the human figures. We slip through the holes, more than happy. Down and
through all of it again, forever.

A SINISTER TIME OF IT WAS HAD BY ALL

Hee, hee, hee. And your cousin, the Mole.

A MUSEUM OF MAKING DO

When all was said and done the human parts were my favorites.
Sun glints through glass roofs under which someones move, irregularly
ambulant. I'm glad we never make it to the mall, in the dream that ends
the instant before we kiss. We kiss and kiss, pretty kissing. Parts move
smooth, through the meanings.

FILM NOIR

Physical fusion found us sprawled, quiet in the smoking dark,
cool-tangled sheets, all pulsing skin. Smell of close, of hair.
Two stilllwarm bodies breathe without underwear. Moist city vacancy
blows an extended kiss.

ROTATIONS NOTED

When one still-visible selfhood first briefly stared then almost smiled
at another still-visible selfhood, I smiled too. Nothing was piercing the sun,
no claw, no tempest. Then somebody had the bright idea of trying to levitate
a table, raise the dead. I stared into the smiling-at, so I still smiled too.
Such turns took place all throughout the night of the winter of the body,
a waltz everyone somehow got invited to, where things are crystal clear.

AN INCOMPLETELY-BRIGHT SCIENZA

We're not refrains, in any case. And how do you like it down here
in the dew and dark, gelatinous grasses. Fine. That's just as well.
But hold on, let's shiver off this particular stage-set and make way
for different quarters altogether, stations a map told me once, we
may be reached from there. Again and again made to remember
matter is what we are and are in, in and out of sound.

ON THE ECHOING SCENE

There were sudden stops at ice cream shops, and such-like. And friendly
down here, really friendly with the voices. They will never stop, they never stop saying.
And deepdown no-one directly wants them to, ever.
I remember a body sprawled in a car, where the head was had opened up.
These scenes spattered with all manner of matters and means.

SUNSHINE PROSTHETIC

Today's remains stand upon the virtues of stretching the truth,
the idea of truth, that gold throat. We liked you as sunlight,
liked your whims, they destroyed us in the end, which was pretty grand.
Clearly this lunacy must stop, but not until it's all inclined toward the stars,
bodies touching bodies in every conceivable way.

PLYING THE VINES

Depending on the crescendo, we could be found out, you know. That might be
in the end a good thing, but who's to say. We sit at table together, grin and lick,
salt and sweat, undressing the music bit by bit.

Succulences of all sorts made gradually everything change. You held a mirror
to my mirror, in a dream. Storms are departing now. What remains remains
and it's our game to name the chaos and the speckles.

To give a human face to change, as I said. By the way, I'll have you know that
prophecy allows for it, I've read up. And then there goes the wind: again
and again, you and I furiously involved and involving.

A PARTIAL UNITY

As when the lines of a body entwine tendrilous with the curlings of another body's
lines. Thought at times was play, no-one could touch harm unless they cared to.
A pulse, vinelike, writhing up in just-dawn. And the wind goes down
down and in, and the last thing, the wind goes.

HOME

Some people felt like places on the street. We met there often, day was glad
though hard. Difficult to understand or for that matter withstand the straining through
to touch. Until what's beneath us, supporting us, divides again, grids
shift, hexes fail, weathervanes are removed all across the mid-west, and once more
we're taken whither we wouldst not have gone. Something understands. Our sun-skins
subdividing, join every weather once again.

AWAY

Childlike and vengeful, storms have continually taken away and up our tents
and best laid plans. Every last one of us, you can bet, is serious about this sort of ceiling
or ending to our erstwhile and rather voluptuous circus, complete
with side-shows, show-down, and remove. Last thing to do at the old junction
when push was shoved, was to plant mirrors in the angles made by the dividing roads,
have everything branching glass.

PRIMUM MOBILE

Simple slashmarks are the best way to begin, to simply begin,
whether the frame is something to wonder at or play violently in
behind the dints by which you change, where before and after fuse.
I like us best when lightning comes, plains to the south and west of here
spread out, endless ripplings purpling into haze: that way to see through
slashmarks in the storm.

EXEUNT ALL

This part's terrific, really terrific. Somewhere and meanwhile,
names are baying other names. Trees branch, leaves turn, time dies,
and so on. The question before us today is, as you guessed, can there really come
no final thing. Naturally all that follows follows from the first
continuance here. So when we get to where the end would have been, it's the view
from there. Beyond that, words won't have much to do with it.

CREDO

To do a kind of green and dangling nondamage to language. Spark of the superflux, mark X on the bottom of the sea. Make little airholes in doubt.

DAWN WIND

A spiraling sign widens upwards. The development is positive, no dust mote missing. Your eyes somewhere open blink as the wind picks up.

HORIZON EVENT

Not a form of thought but thinking. Skin breathes, uneven. They let you lie in a place where a sense of suddenly violent freedom pervades.

THREE PORTRAITS

All about the wet-bright house a double rainbow came, have you ever seen one, it failed to be dull as did mostly we. Things underneath or between it were done, as ever, long before and after it was gone, but not from our spotty memories. What was made up above the grass and grass-like stitches, all up and down the sides of our arms. Playthings they have claws and teeth and stop to look at you once or twice before it's finished. No more hesitation in the perfectly circular drops still hanging in the air as we reel back outside the glistening house.

You get on a bus. It turns out, since you and he are alone and end up talking, that the bus driver is actually the mayor of a small nearby town. January outside. By now the bus feels like an enormous barn hurtling down a cushioned road. The bus driver, the mayor, has a bus driver's haircut. He drives right by your stop, assuming you go to college in the town and thus do not wish to go home. You are and were more like the flickering snowfields adrift outside this moving barn than you were or are the person going home. Which is when the mayor cracks a smile or even laughs. Nothing but what's up ahead, in the mirrors of his shades.

My face is pretty large, red, round, and seeming. I look therefore like the sun. We're not in any way to be demarcated, to be worked out. Something wet twisting thrives in first, earliest-rooted places. There were those who wanted to take us away from us but we would not let them, except sometimes in the dark, when everything listened and was unclearly leafy and creeping. You and I are our skins, having invaginated into organs, fluid systems, kinds of seeming. First and last places, bloodtrees in the brain, behind and between which hide other people entirely, other people at all.

SPECKLED ARRANGEMENTS

Facts are closely pinned. We need to soften keeping, no mathematized wax. And the very next day you brought me flowers. That's it, keep the ceiling moving until the mix of blues and whites is just right. Amid doing this and that are meaningful, however simple or complex, mechanisms. Here are the springs that connect two wooden pistil-and-stamen arrangements for instance. Events themselves were something else, really something else inside. Our garden held so many rain-receiving open throats and tongues.

Nobodies sang best, and multiply, at that. Small mirrors blew leaflike up and down front halls. Wind is only the traces of wind, anyway, no matter. Little candle lit inside the throat. And whatever gathers listening there—when the rainbirds came from behind a glass partition into this very room in a gust of redgreen dartings, one felt at home. Whole body open, briefly receiving lives from without.

A relative calm settled over the escarpment. At least no-one would be visiting soon. Drifts of mist in the trees and so on could be found, entertained. There's always time for infinite games. X stands for former, plus a kiss. The tattered rest of the treasure-map must've fallen out of my pocket on the way, I'm not sure, though I hope better when you are. Sometimes when what happens happens, like the day you and I lay down in the middle of a rural road in beginning rain, we come here glad to be afraid.

HOMO SAPIEN

Today back then I have one white eyebrow hair. And my clothes are not
of the most kind, too many patches. Body makes its last glance like the first,
there is no last. Something twisting, in here, behind its eyes. Glad to be born among
the swallowing-feeling things, nothing's ragged, nothing torn.
At one point we lie down like dominoes in a maze, astonished to be falling
productively. Then skin convulses beyond pleasure, inside a star implodes.

WHAT THE LAUGHTER SAID

for Fanny Howe

Line and form magnify glass. Some kind of setup down by the woods,
a few thrown flares, and we're sure. Here are rivulets across and through
downwardly decomposing layers of leaves. Light moves too soon, it says.
Everything's a butterfly flickering over darkening flowers.

IN WHICH SAD LIGHT / A CARVÉD DOLPHIN SWAM

Costumes make a dance complete. Disguise your insides, when you need.
Shift and play. A door was talking down a long hallway to a window which decided
it wasn't saying much of anything at all, something about or like the noise of wind,
medium of speech.

THAT'S THAT

We're gone down the dawn wind. Words answer this, in them I can think
I am. You said it best yourself. I loved running through the branches,
when it matters anymore. One dies, another dies, another one dies, and
meanwhile everything happens, somewhere between being and seeming,
in a mindless wind.

THAT'S WHAT YOU THOUGHT

But it wasn't very effective in the end, was it, except for getting you out of sundry
necessary services, for which we are ever glad. Guns keep going off,
there are bells inside my head. One can bear only so much futility, you know.
This time I spent listening to the human voice in all its forms, spent completely
listening, carving a hearing, including this.

AS IF SOMETHING BURST

I'm a toy on a talking stick, beneath the couch. Patterns can be fun
to play in the dark, when senses bend back toward the head sometimes.
Anywhere outside is only further invitation to move at this point,
but for the rain. Animals' faces blur when it rains and rains and I am sick
of this rain, says the stick.

AMONG THE FINAL PLAYTHINGS

Small performances motioned in the dark. To do what we had to feeling
was a need. Pinioned and purposed, torsos arched in the air. Clover had kids,
cousins ate. Apart from the fact of our imminent departures were even smaller
wilier entrances and exits and cloud-appearances, all of which we forged,
through which we work our way.

III.

FORMAL ENTRIES & HORN O' PLENTY

DAY-FRAME, SKY BLUE, SUN BLAZING

It's marvelous, inviting guests from a distance! Come in
to this hovel or handbuilt dustplace, please welcome. Here

the room is spread all over, you can go anywhere, be anything,
any number of old or new or nonselves again, as you like.

Facing these mirrors are pools: blue-lit waterripples reflected
in sloweddown burned sand curved, then framed. Naturally

these scenes mix, even at a molecular level. Soon come
mutations in thought that mean more than we could think before.

MY NAME IS MUD

The first person pronoun, that gallows, is always both available and variable.
I am the one who took your purse or wallet, yes. Crowds bulge by; ones known under
another sun, a sign. So reinvent the wheel, if it pleases you
feelingly. Such a pleasure to make mouths such as these among the meanings.

Little possibilities come out sideways, at times. When I begin the story
of my life I say, "At first, an ache. Then from it came something, which
in the gnarlingly rootlike course of time turned out to be me. Or call itself
me, instead of other kinds of things." And so on, indefinitely.

CUT IT ALL OUT IN LITTLE STARS

Insert human insight here, and here,
and here, you get the point. Ha-ha. [Quick, this grows old:

"spooky music" ensues.] Wow, how you've changed! Is it a good thing,
like the sky? Is the radio OK, to watch, I mean?

Significant glances can, naturally and or artificially, be exchanged,
but only at exactly *right* times of day.

Plus all those nights you were alone in yourself like a goldfish in a green bowl,
yuck. Well,

Ohio sounds good to me. Prettymuch anywhere
but here. So why did you originally want to go, again?

Whether or not the weather'll matter's another issue entirely,
I assure you.

All things ebb and flow. We have fins and spines, and can prove
capable of coming through conversations at an almost infinite

remove, so what's the point, the glimmer? Ah,
to mime a return to knowing again and again and again.

MEAT SONG

Beginning.

Some consternation down here in the sun sometimes, as nearby human frames smear from the edges, rough-hewn as they are, of this our first and final hunching in the light.

Middle.

Outside: city-rain. Right now I hear the neighbors fucking.
The lady yells.

End.

Tray, Blanch, and Sweetheart come, let's suggest our own kind of storm.

HUMAN WEATHER

A strikingly forked sort of governance your orders
wield, 'til you name the nothing
at war with the nothing inside (as they say) you.

*

We're sculpted, stucco'd indeed; other lives, other things extrude.
Carbon forms. Erosion signs. Diamond rings.

*

(While Willy will yellow away, May may remain May.)

FIGURE STUDY

A person paints a house on fire. There is a house on fire.

A person's paint makes a house of fire move and more. Okay.

Something in the person's house must be on fire, by the look of the way
it curls, crackling.

Paint makes backdrops to many kinds of fires, always has. Think: caves.

Our person isn't listed in the phonebook, nor, locally anyway, listened to much.

[c.f., The person who cried Fire] [A spreading person.]

In a house-painting a fire-person [insert molten mirrors here]
smears blurs of mirror-people

in the cackling flames coming now clearly, quite volubly,
from a smouldering frame [a mirror-few unnamed waving,

weeping, kissing each & every one of the tongues of fire Goodbye.]

AND WHILE YOU'RE AT IT, HAVE A NICE DAY

in the wire-and-daisy-veined though resolutely-nonabhorrent vacuum known as now

MANIFESTUS

When they come to sequence you, to tell you
how and when and precisely why to divide
don't let them, is my advice. *You are the orchestra*

and its pit, don't let the bastards try to come arrange
the music your knowing is. Since everyone
in the listening arena is also capable of being
approached by phone at apparently any

even every time of day considering
the weather and all, it's enough to make you stop
speaking to people forever! But then there's the itch,

series of cellular events roughly described as affection
in aftertime. For now you move on amid the blood,
the little and large amounts of daily blood through human
wires, where it was not your place to be animal here

in the first place, stuck listening to so many of your own
murders day in day out; why not say what you will.
You will.

GREEN THOUGHT, GREEN SHADE

for Josh Corey

I have to wait 'til the goddamned trees speak to me
before I can go on, you know, proceed.

Giddy to go by, I ride and ride and ride
'til the sun or something of the sort takes me down.

Do la-la, I do la-la by the brook. Fusky stuff.
Ripples in puddles, or nerves on a surface, slow.

We go down to soon go by. We go by and by.
Weeds wreck an angle I am taking to arrive

somewhere close to here, transformed, among friends.
Another self, another time of day, another sound.

AS SUN WAS SETTING

I forgot the glass of water that was sitting on the table.
I forgot the glass of water that was sitting, standing, or lying on the table.
The table stood squarely on the floor, of course, far above which
I was the observer, I saw the whole event

that moment was, and to tell the truth thoroughly I enjoyed
its branchings out. Just as I turned
to come into this room now and write this I remembered that
I forgot the glass of water that was anywhere on the table;

it was where it was, naturally, but I couldn't see it from where I was
because as I said I was busy turning away from the table
standing in the kitchen on which the glass darkly, clearly sang
of days gone by and to come. I was, however, not too busy

away-turning to notice this and listen, half-laughing by then
further on somewhere, alive to having been here.

FORMAL ENTRY

Me sign hello. I say sign, sign again.

You've got what it takes.

Your vehicle will be arriving soon, never fear.

There are still many things to do around the house.

[Something missing here.]

It's all going to be a great success, I assure you.

Luck and time are on your side, as ever.

Spiritual weapons, spiritual weapons, don't forget.

Ho ho ho, haa ha ha, hee hee hee . . . . Oh—sign again

please if you don't mind so I can make sure it's

really you. OK, thanks again

for all your support throughout the years.

Something moving through the clouds.

Is there any pain, where you are still. Sign here.

Thanks, and hello again.

HORN O'PLENTY,

or, NOTES TOWARD A SUPREME CORNUCOPIA

DEDICATED TO EVERY
SINGLE PERSON WHO HAS
EXISTED OR WILL EVER
EXIST ON THE EARTH

AND I MEAN IT

EPIGRAPH TO POEM:

"I'M JUST BEING
WHAT I MEAN

HERE
TOO BELIEVE
ME"

*

1.

IF IMAGINARY FRIENDS DIDN'T EXIST
I would have to invent them

HURRAH it is Spring
Time again in antiheroic couplettings

In Ithacan air

JEEZ! What a real
Piece of work is man, is woman! I mean

2.

Actual pieces of actual work.

You'll hear it
when you
know it, it's
a Real Hoot

YEAH BUT WHAT'S A RIVER

UTTER BLASPHEMY

A MORNING ROMP

3.

PUTTING A LIEN ON NEVERLAND

ALL THE TRICKS EVIL COULD
DO ON HIS GLIMMERY MOTORIZED
BICYCLE, HIS TWO-WHEELER, WHOO

THEY TRIED TO SHOOT HIM

4.

out of the air with an
anti-aircraft gun. Today the river still snakes on.

PLAYING TO THE PEANUT GALLERY

TAKING A PISS ON A PILE OF URINAL ICE IN DUBLIN

5.

JUST OFF THE HIGHWAY
FROM THE PLACE DOWN
THE ROAD FROM
HERE FEWER
PEOPLE TAKE

YOU'RE BEING REDUNDANT,

6.

He shouted, You're just
Saying the same thing

Over and over again
Day in day out!

WARFARE CLASS

THESE CLOUDS ARE TERRIFIC

7.

THAT MOVIE WAS SO BAD
IT MADE MY FRIEND
LAUGH AT A GENOCIDE

FREE BONDAGE

TO BE AND NOT TO BE
NO QUESTION ABOUT IT

SHADOWPEOPLE PEEK THROUGH
OUR WOOD-AND-GLASS BOXES

8.

Try to keep your
Sink clean

Please mind the wild
Animals, not-so-distant,
Who'd like nothing
Better than to devour
You in an incredibly
Messy series of graceful
Relentless attacks.

GROUND NEEDS FOOD

9.

ON the WORSHIP of
SKELETONS in this nation
And why those krazy kidz
Try to emulate them

WEATHER RETORT

A CLEAN, WELL-LIGHTED
AUTOMATON

10.

PHOTOGENESIS, or,
AS LUCK WOULD HAVE IT

INFINITE MACRAMÉ

You, wallflower, come
Back here and dance
In the absence of grace

SWIMMING POLL

11.

WILL THE REAL [Insert Poet Laureate here]
PLEASE STAND UP

IS THERE ANYONE IN THE AUDIENCE
FROM [in this case, TED KOOSER]? IF SO PLEASE APPLAUD

IS THERE A HOUSE
IN THE DOCTOR

MICE NEVER LAY PLANS
THEY'RE BETTER PEOPLE
THAN THAT

12.

PORTRAIT OF PRE-RAIN AIR

HEARING SOUNDS OUT

I miss my friends
With all my hearts
With all the parts
Of the hearts
Of my hands

AUTOBIOGRAPHY OF A GHOST
OF A FLEA

Chairs are careful

SOFT PARTINGS

13.

BOULDER, CAVE, SHROUD

BODYPRINTS, SOUNDWAVES

*

EVERYTHING DEPENDS
UPON HOW

YOU SPATIALIZE
A SENTENCE

AN ANTHROPOGRAPHIA
FOR

LOBSTERS UNITE
NEURAL NETWORKS UNITE
FINGERSLIKE

EVERYTHING UNITE
WHILE WE'RE AT IT

14.

I think I know
That all we

Know is think,

Which is why
My I am is me.

STUDY FOR A GLASS MASQUESELF
HO

REQUIEM FOR
EVERYBODY

EVIDENTLY X.
DOES NOT SHIT
IN THE WOODS
(WHERE THAT
SORT OF THING'S
ALLOWED)

15.

Pistils & stamens!
Pistils & stamens!

JIGGLY

TOO MUCH DEPENDS
UPON A NONBIG NONRED
NONBARN

HOLD
THE CHICKENS

HOLD
THE WHITE CHICKENS

16.

MONOLOGICALLY SPEAKING

IN DEFENSE OF POLYTHEISM

SOME OF MY BEST FRIENDS ARE ANIMALS

EXPERIMENT RHYTHMS
HESITATION'S THOUGHT IF YOU USE IT

SEE A RAINSPOT RUN

A TOMB BENEATH A MULTINATIONAL
RESTAURANT RUN BY AN
HERMAPHRODITIC CLOWN (LOOK CLOSE, KIDS!)

17.

LEVIT(ATIONALIT)Y

LIGHTNESS HEAVEN-HAVEN

SOMETHING DEAD STUCK IN
WITH LITTLE DRIED FLOWER STEMS & FEATHERS
IN VANISHING DAYLIGHT FULL SUN
STILL HERE NOW

LAW IS SUBTLY SANCTIONED TORTURE

JOBS, HABITS, ROUTINES. YOUR
BODY IS NOT YOUR ARM.

POEMS NEAR DOG WORSHIP
FROM CATLIKE PERSPECTIVES

BOGEY HAS MUCH SWEET MOXIE

AND MOXIE IS WHAT
WE SPOTTED NEED

DEERLY

18.

ON THE ART OF BEING LUMINOUS AT TWILIGHT,
BRIGHT SPECKS REMAIN IN EVERYWHERE,
SQUID'S-INK-BLUE, SHOT THROUGH WITH SOON

LOVELY IDIOT, SAY ON IN WIND

ACTUALLY *SAY* LA VIE

POSTULATIONS IN THE BACK SEAT

A VACANCY OF MOTELS
IN THESE WOODS

19.

HELLISH TOUPÉE

GRAVITY'S GOT ME DOWN

IN NATURE IS NO MURDER

LIFE SENTENCES

STOP BEFORE YOU THINK

THEN G'HEAD

20.

ELEGY FOR THE LIVING

ANTLERED SPECIES BEHIND
AND BEYOND THIS BACKGROUND

DUM-DE-DUM-DUM
DRUMS A SENSE OF
COMING THUNDER

21.

13 INNOCENTS

MERCURIOUS

TEACHING SCHOOL WHAT TO DO

22.

SCATALOGICAL WARFARE, PT. II

TO SEE AGAIN THE DEAD
SINGING IN THE DAWN

WHERE FOR NOW FROM WHEN

23.

IT'S THE WORST JOB
IN THE GOVERNMENT:
EVERYBODY HATES YOU
AND YOU CAN DO NOTHING.

POETRY FOETRY SCHMOETRY BLOWETRY
THOETRY

KNOWETRY

K NO WE TRY

THE LIE-NOEM

BLANK HEARSE, OR, HEARSAY

24.

MOISTURE WHIP

DON'T TAKE YOUR PUNS TO TOWN, BILL

CLOWNS ARE NOT
A DESTRUCTIVE FORCE

WHERE FOR NOW
AND THEN

SOMETHING VOMITED
THE COSMOS, SOMETHING

GORGEOUS, LIKE ANOTHER
COSMOS

25.

IT IS MY DUTY
TO HATE WAR
BECAUSE I'M
STILL ALIVE

LOAFING IS NOT JUST AN ARTFORM,
IT IS ARTFORM

A CERTAIN SLANT
OF LOAF

O SOKRATES, LOQUACIOUS GOAT

STEPPING IN THE SAME FUCKING
RIVER TWICE IN FACT
ANY NUMBER OF TIMES
EVERY BLOODY DAY

HEM A GLOBE IN

26.

THINGS ACCORDIAN IN AND OUT, CORNUCOPEALATING

CONTRACTS EXPAND

COYOTE WAKING, COYOTE FALLING ASLEEP,
COYOTE COHABITATING BRIEFLY
WHAT'S LEFT OF US

NAMES'RE MOSTLY ASH IN AIR

BODY MAKES
SENSE

PLURAL BELLS, LABIALATIONS BLOOM

27.

MY NAME IS MARK
ALWAYS HAS BEEN

KARL WAS JUST
A LARK

PRISONS SHOULD BE OUTLAWED

IF THE DUST
ON THESE SHOES
COULD TALK
IT WOULD
PREFER TO SAY
NOTHING AND
TO SAY NOTHING
PRECISELY AND

MULTIPLY IN
FACT

28.

YOU MADE YOUR WORLD
NOW SLEEP WITH IT

APRIL IS NATIONAL
CRUELTY MONTH

TUBERS UNITE, YOUR
EYES EXTEND PINK
AND FINGERLIKE INTO
DARK AND ARE THUS
BIOLOGICAL INSPIRATION
FOR ALL WHO DWELL
HOW DEEP THERE

29.

THROATSPLINTER

SELF-PORTRAIT AS SOMETIMES-FRIGHTENED

MANNEQUINS MAKE DO,
MAKE PEOPLE DO
THINGS IN THE STREET

DODO & GIGI & TREE

30.

FIRSTAWHILE
FEELINGHOME

WE LEARN TO
MOVE AMONG
OTHER PEOPLE

AND THINGS NO
DOUBT FULL OF
DOUBT AT TIMES

STILL MOVING

31.

FORM'S NIGHTMARE'S
CONTENT'S DREAM

THE JURORS START
TO FILE IN, ALL
THE STOCK GENERALITIES
IN PLAY

COYOTE SEES LENNY,
FOUR RAISED EYEBROWS THINKING

32.

ANIMÉ MIME

GOITER OPERATIONS

ENNUI IS NOT
REALLY A WORD

I DEDICATE FISH-STICKS TO THEMSELVES

AND TO WILL, TO
HUMAN VOLITION

33.

NO-ONE'S ONUS

TIME, IT TURNS OUT
[SOMETHING MISSING HERE]

*

34.

REPRISE OR REPRIEVE
YOU PICK

NOTES OF THE MEMBRANE
OF A CELL WHOSE CENTER
IS NOWHERE & WHOSE VOLUME
INFINITELY EXPANDS

0

THE DREAM
WAS THAT
WE THOUGHT
WE COULD
THINK WE
COULD THINK

ARRIVING EVERYWHERE
IN MATERIAL WAVES
CONTINUALLY INVOLUTING

I IS A SKIN

35.

YOU JUST GOTTA
STRIKE LIGHTNING
WHILE IRON RINGS

THIS TITLE IS A LITTLE BIT
OF A LONG TITLE, ALL GUARANTEED
TO TITTLE, Piddle, clink.

36.

A MESSAGE
FROM BEING
TO BEING
ABOUT BEING

37.

LINES CAN'T HAVE TITLES
VISUAL EVENTS ENOUGH
TO MAKE MOUTHS OF
& AT & FROM

MY NEW TWO FAVORITE
WORDS ARE POTENTIALLY
INFINITE

38.

THIS AND ALL THAT
IT IMPLIES DOES
HAPPEN TO BE

THE CASE IN WHICH
MY WORKS UNFURL

CHURL MEET MOUNTEBANK
MOUNTEBANK MEET ERL-KING

ANTLERED LAUGHTER

DUMB INFINITE BLIND VIOLENT LOVING IRRITATED
WORLD WORLD WORLD

39.

JUGGLE GRINS AND WINCES

GREENOPEN DIARY OF A FIFTH LEVEL PALINDROME

GOING, GOING, GONG

I CAN'T EVEN MENACE
THE GHOST IF I TRY

I JUST NOW REALIZED
WHAT I'M DOING COMPLETELY
AND THAT'S ALWAYS FUN

40.

THREE FEATHERS
THREE THINGS THAT INFORMED YOU
THREE IMAGES FROM YOUR ARM

WHO LIVES

41.

LET'S FACE IT
OR RATHER

LET'S LET IT
FACE ME WITH

THE FACT THAT
I CAN'T KEEP

WRITING THESE
THINGS ON POST-

ITS FUCKING
FOREVER NOW

CAN I

[POEM ENDS HERE, OR,
AT LAST, MANUSCRIPT BREAKS OFF]

OBVIOUS APOCRYPHA

HURM STURM

POSTHUMOUS ANYHOWS

CURA ANIMARUM

READ MY PS'S, A LETTER IN MANY NOVELS

READ MY TONGUE: NO NEW WAGES OF SIN!

HOME FROM JAIL COME

LIFE IS BUT
A BIT A FISH

WE MUST LOVE EACH OTHER
AND DIE, OR WHATEVER

SNOW FALLS ONLY ON THE LIVING, JIM

TERPSICHORE

WE ARE
WHAT WE

DWELL ON
& IN

HORNO OR CUERNO

AS EVER
AS IS

*

NOTES & ACKNOWLEDGEMENTS

The epigraphs are from *Judy*—a 1994 installation by artist Tony Oursler at the Institute of Contemporary Art in Philadelphia, Aristotle's *History of Animals* and Percy Shelley's *A Defence of Poetry*.

"RESURRECTION OF THE DEAD" is a collage: pieces from the Bible interwoven with testimonial excerpts from Géza Róheim's *Magic and Schizophrenia* (1955).

Some of the poems in this book have appeared in *Fence, Seneca Review, Downtown Brooklyn, No Tell Motel, Spoon River, the tiny, Gedankenstrich* (Berlin), *Eleven Bulls, can we have our ball back?* and *Mipoesias*.

Thanks and more than thanks to all who played parts in the life that made these poems: Karen Leona Anderson, Jasper Bernes, Cybele Berret, Dwight Codr, Josh Corey, Gina Franco, Jerry Gabriel, Roger Gilbert, Reesa Grushka, Gabe Gudding, Will Hacker, Fanny Howe, Paul Jaskunas, David Lehman, Gina Myers, Carly Sachs and Bill van Esveld.

To Sarah Ferguson-Wagstaffe, such a marvelous, lovely friend. Thank you.

My gratitude to Reb Livingston for believing in my work, and for her insight and patience.

To Bill Ecenbarger, dear brother & friend, without whom I wouldn't be.

And to Ivy Kleinbart, more than words can say.

Thou drewest near in the day

ABOUT THE AUTHOR

Author Photo:
Ivy Kleinbart

Karl Parker is from Lock Haven, Pennsylvania. After graduate studies at Cornell and the New School's writing program, he won the 2004 Poetry Award and the Dorothy & Sidney Willner Literary Scholarship Award from the National Arts Club Literary Committee. Having taught at Hunter College, Cornell, and Auburn Correctional Facility (unfortunately the site of the first electric chair execution in 1890), he currently teaches literature and creative writing at Hobart and William Smith Colleges.

ALSO BY NO TELL BOOKS

2010

God Damsel, by Reb Livingston
Crushes, by Lea Graham
Glass is Really a Liquid, by Bruce Covey

2008

Cadaver Dogs, by Rebecca Loudon

2007

The Bedside Guide to No Tell Motel - 2nd Floor, editors Reb Livingston
      & Molly Arden
Harlot, by Jill Alexander Essbaum
Never Cry Woof, by Shafer Hall
Shy Green Fields, by Hugh Behm-Steinberg
The Myth of the Simple Machines, by Laurel Snyder

2006

The Bedside Guide to No Tell Motel, editors Reb Livingston & Molly Arden
Elapsing Speedway Organism, by Bruce Covey
The Attention Lesson, by PF Potvin
Navigate, Amelia Earhart's Letters Home, by Rebecca Loudon
Wanton Textiles, by Reb Livingston & Ravi Shankar

notellbooks.org

CPSIA information can be obtained
at www.ICGtesting.com
Printed in the USA
LVHW061618230221
679745LV00031B/1059